EVERYDAY

CORNISH

by

Rod Lyon

A Pocket-book

to teach yourself colloquial Cornish

without all that grammar

Published by Dyllansow Truran
Trewolsta, Trewirgie, Redruth, Kernow (Cornwall)
Printed by Short Run Press Ltd., Exeter

DYLLANSOW TRURAN
ISBN 0 907566 78 2

Everyday Cornish

Everyday Cornish has been designed for those readers whose main desire is to speak the language yet who do not wish to, or cannot, get to grips with pages of seemingly endless grammar.

There are many books on the market which to the academically minded are invaluable, in that they provide and explain every aspect of the language enabling him to produce good **literary** Cornish. However, these books fail to achieve the one really important factor concerning minority languages - the presentation of the language to the man in the street, the mr. Average who is ultimately responsible for its survival.

It is to this mr. Average that **Everyday Cornish** is aimed - providing a working Cornish that will enable him to join in a conversation and make himself understood - yet not involving him in the study of complicated grammar. Of course, certain points have to be explained, but these are kept to a bare minimum. The Cornish itself is simple and **colloquial**, this being an integral part of the living language.

Some advice on using this book.

- Master each page before turning to the next. Follow the sentence patterns given and construct your own based on these, introducing new topics and words to give you a broader understanding and better command of the language.

- Practise **regularly**. It is far more rewarding to spend a short time **everyday** studying than to try and undergo long but infrequent sessions. This only clogs and tires the brain.

- use the language whenever and wherever possible. Meet Cornish speakers, join in 'Yeth an Weryn' groups. Cornish like any other language is there to be **used** - not learnt about.

Rod Lyon

Pronunciation.

The Unified Spelling system introduced earlier this century and which is currently used throughout the Cornish-English and English-Cornish dictionaries has been adopted in this book.

This system was devised to rid the written language of earlier irregularities in spelling, but unfortunately over the years it induced a change in the pronunciation of the spoken word. Many vowel and consonant sounds which differ slightly from one onother were, in the creation of the Unified System, all grouped together and given one representative character. Consequently those wishing to learn Cornish from the written word cannot through this system expect to correctly pronounce, **not taking into consideration dialect**, much of the language.

However in an attempt to combat this failing, accents as employed in the dictionaries have been used over the vowels, but it should be noted that these are not included in the general writing of the Language.

In addition when a word is colloquially different from that represented by the dictionary form, an English 'phonetic' spelling has been included alongside. For example, the letter 's' in the dictionary has sounds which vary from 'z' through 's' to 'j' ('Wosa' in dictionary, pronounced 'Wuja')

Key to Pronunciation

Vowels

single

a	short	as a in man	y	short	as y in rhythm.
ā	long	between ε in wet and ai in bait	ȳ	long	as εε in seen.
ε	short	as ε in pen			
ε̃	long	as ai in rain			
o	short	as o in pot			
ō	long	as aw in dawn			
u	short	as u in full			
ü	between ou in you and εε in meet				
ū	long	as u in use			

2.

Vowels. Double

ay }	as y in my but	ew	as ew in dew
ey }	with slight dipthong.	ou	as ou in you
		ow	as ow in cow

aw   as **ow** in owl

eu   between vowel sound
     doe & **dew**

Consonants

Single

b   as in English

c   always hard as
    in cat.

d   as in English

f   as in fan, but lightly
    sounded at end of word.

g   always hard as in get

h   as in hat, but lightly
    sounded in the middle
    of word

j   as in jug

k   as in king

l   as l in bolt or
    ll in bullet

m }
n }
p } as in English
r }

s   as in salt

t   before **a,c,o,r,u** as
    t in table; before y
    close to sound of ch
    in church.

v   as in English

w   as in wet

y   as in yes

Double

bm } voiced as one
dn } without any vowel
     sound coming
     between them.

● These combinations are
colloquial and not found
in the dictionaries. They
occur only in mono-syllables
and accentuated syllables.

ch as in chapel

dh as th in there

th as th in thin

ll stronger than l,
    approaching sound of
    li in valiant.

qu as in quarter

sh as in shop

wh as in white but
    strong h sound.

gh strong h sound

gw as in gwen

gwl) at the beginning of
gwr (words there is only
wl (a slight sound of the
wr) w before the l & r

● Note, 'th' at the end of words is very often silent
   e.g. 'forth' is pronounced 'for'.

● The dialect of West Penwith will give the correct
   sounds for the foregoing (particularly the vowels)
   and should be adhered to as closely as possible.

Where you are; what you are doing.

statements

1

theram	= I am
theros	= you are (sing.)
mava	= he is
ma-hӳ	= she is
ma'n den	= the man is
ma Jowan	= John is
ma'n fleghes	= the children are
theron	= we are
therough	= you are (plur.)
theronjӳ	= they are

2

ow ponya	= running
ow tybry	= eating
owth eva	= drinking
ow cül	= making
ow kerdhes	= walking
ow cana	= singing
ow quary	= playing
ow mōs	= going
ow tōs	= coming
ow redya	= reading

3

yn	= in
war	= on
dhe	= to
dadn	= under
tewa	= towards
orth	= at
obma	= here
ena	= there

4

an chӳ	= the house
an gegyn	= the kitchen
an lowarth	= the garden
an drē	= the town
an darras	= the door
an kyttryn	= the bus

5

lebmyn	= now
haneth	= tonight
yn lent	= slowly
yn üskys	= quickly
hedhyu	= today
yn ta	= well

● Note in column 2, 'ow' becomes 'owth' before vowels.

● 'Yn an' becomes y'n' — e.g. ' Y'n chӳ = 'In the house.' 'Dhe a' becomes 'dhe'n' — e.g. 'dhe'n' drē = 'to the town'.

● There is no word for 'a' in Cornish, i.e. 'chӳ' = a house

● Nouns in Cornish are either masculine or feminine, but don't worry about this yet.

Now from the above columns make as many easy sentences as you can, using the following combinations:-
1+2 ; 1+2+3+4; 1+2+3+4+5; 1+3+4 ; 1+3+4+5. For example:-

1+2: Theram ow mōs = I am going.
1+2+3+4: Ma'n dēn ow tybry y'n gegyn = The man is eating in the kitchen.
1+2+3+4+5: Ma-hy ow cana y'n drē hedhyu = She is singing in the town today.
1+3+4: Ma Jowan orth an darras = John is at the door.
1+3+4+5: Theronjӳ y'n lowarth lebmyn = they are in the
        (loor)   garden now.

4.

● Column 2 can be followed by a **Noun object** before continuing with columns 3, 4 and 5.
e.g.

'Theram ow cül **mōs** y'n gegyn' = 'I am making a
                                          table in the kitchen.'

more words for you to construct sentences with.

Nouns			
an lyver	= the book	an bōs	= the food
an lyfrow	= the books	on amary	= the cupboard
mowes	= a girl	an gwely	= the bed
an vowes	= the girl	mōs	= a table
an vowysy	= the girls	an vōs	= the table
benen	= a woman	an stevel	= the room
an venen	= the woman	an desen	= the cake
an benenes	= the women	an kēs	= cheese

Verbs			
ow quertha	= selling	owth ōla	= crying
ow codha	= falling	ow pōbas	= baking
ow crambla	= climbing	ow prenasa	= shopping
ow carma	= shouting	ow tōn	= carrying
ow wherthyn	= laughing	ow cuska	= sleeping
ow labma	= jumping	ow fysky	= rushing

● Learn the foregoing and master the construction of the sentences before moving on. The present tense given here is the basic pattern for the other most common tenses.

Negatives
          This is very easy for you now that you have learnt the basic pattern. Simply alter **Column 1** to the following.

Nyns eram	=	I am not
Nyns erosta	=	you are not (sing.)
Nyns üsy-va (ejy va)	=	he is not
Nyns üsy-hȳ (ejy hȳ)	=	she is not
Nyns üsy an dēn	=	the man is not
Nyns üsy Jowan	=	John is not
Nyns üsy an fleghes	=	the children are not
Nyns eronȳ	=	we are not
Nyns erough-whȳ	=	you are not (plur.)
Nyns eron-jȳ	=	they are not

Now join these to the combinations as before, e.g.

1+2+3+4: 'Nyns eram ow quary y'n gegyn' = 'I am not
playing in the kitchen'.

1+3+4: 'Nyns ùsy-va war an kyttryn' = 'He is not on the bus.'

> • 'Nyns ùsy.....' is used when there is a definite
> subject, i.e.
> 'He is not.....'; 'She is not....'; 'John is not......'.
> When an indefinite subject is governing the
> clause, then 'Nyns ùsy' is replaced by 'Nyns us'
> e.g., 'a boy is not....'; (really, 'there is'nt a boy)
>
> This will be more obvious when we look at questions.

Questions

Again this is very easy for you. This time
all you have to do is knock off the 'Nyns' in the
negative statement! Thus Column 1 becomes:

eram......?	= am I.......?
erosta...?	= are you.....?
ùsy-va....?	= is he.......?
ùsy-hy.....?	= is she.....?
ùs map....?	= is a boy....?
ùsy Jowan..?	= is John......?
ùsy an dùs...?	= are the men...?
erony.......?	= are we......?
erough-why?	= are you....?
eron-jy......?	= are they....?

Now line these
up with the
other columns
as before, e.g.

'eram ow môs?'
= 'am I going?'

'ùsy-hy y'n lowarth?
= 'is she in the
garden?' etc.

Replies

There is no YES or NO in Cornish as
direct replies to questions. For the Negative reply
we use a slightly amended form of the negative
statement on the previous page, in that 'Nyns' is
replaced by 'Nag' and the little suffix where
joined by a hyphen is generally dropped
Thus: 'Nyns eram' becomes 'Nag eram'.
'Nyns ùsy-va' becomes 'Nag ùsy'

For the affirmative reply simply drop the 'Nag' above.
e.g. 'erosta ow môs?' = 'Are' you going?
'Nag eram' - 'No (I am not)' - 'eram'- 'Yes (I am)'

● Although these are the direct answers to the questions, it is, depending on circumstances, more polite to complete the sentence by repeating the whole statement, be it negative or affirmative.

e.g. 'Ûsy Jowan y'n stevel?' - 'Is John in the room?'
'Nag ûsy, nyns ûsy-va y'n stevel' - 'No, he is not in the room.'
'Ûsy Jory y'n gegyn?' - 'Is George in the kitchen?'
'Ûsy, mava y'n gegyn.' - 'Yes, he is in the kitchen.'

Negative Questions

No problem! Just add 'a' to the start of the negative statement. E.g.
'A nyns ûsy Jowan ow tôs?' - 'Isn't John coming?'
In colloquial Cornish, the 'a' is not always sounded, the tone of the voice being considered sufficient:
'nyns ûsy Jowan ow tôs?'

'Ma' and 'Nyns ûs'
Apart from the meaning already learnt, 'Ma' has two other very useful meanings - **There is** or **There are**.
e.g.
'Ma dên y'n gegyn' - 'There is a man in the kitchen.'
The negative form **There is not, there are not** is given by **Nyns ûs**
e.g.
'Nyns ûs dên y'n gegyn' - 'There is not a man in the kitchen' (i.e. - 'There is no man in the kitchen')
The question is formed as we have already learnt.
e.g.
'Ûs dên y'n gegyn?' - 'Is there a man in the kitchen?'
And of course the replies are carried out in the same way.

Two useful words for Questions :
'Plê' - 'where'; 'P'ûr - 'when'
With 'plê', simply tack it on the front of the affirmative statement in Column I.
e.g. 'Plê theram.....?' - 'Where am I.....?'

With 'p'ûr' it is even easier! Tack it on the question on the previous page.
e.g. 'P'ûr ûsy-va ow tôs?' - 'When is he coming?'

Where you were; what you were doing

statements

Replace Column I this time with the following:

thera vȳ	=	I was
theras ta	=	you were (sing.)
thera va	=	he was
thera hȳ	=	she was
thera an dēn	=	the man was
thera Jowan	=	John was
thera an düs	=	the men were
thera nȳ	=	we were
thera whȳ	=	you were (plur.)
thera an jȳ	=	they were

Negatives

These are simple.
Just replace the
'th' by 'Nyns'
e.g.
'Nyns era vȳ ow mōs'
= 'I was not going'.
'Nyns era an düs ena'
= 'The men were not
    there'.

Questions & Replies

Questions: Even easier! Simply use 'era' etc
without the prefix.
e.g. 'Era Jowan war an kyttryn?' = 'Was John on the bus?'
     'Era an jȳ ow carma?' = 'Were they shouting?'

Replies: As with the present tense, the affirmative
and negative replies are carried out in exactly the same way.
e.g. 'Era va ow kerdhes y'n drē?' = 'Was he walking in the
                    (kerres)   town?'

        'Era.' = 'Yes (he was)'
        'Nag era'. = 'No (he wasn't)'.

● Now compose sentences as before using the
combination of columns.

'Thera' - There was, there were

Like 'Ma', 'thera' has these alternative useful
meanings.
e.g. 'Thera dēn y'n gegyn' = 'There was a man in the
                        kitchen.'
Negative: 'Nyns era' = 'There was not/were not.'
Question: 'Era?' = 'Was/were there?'
    As you would expect, the replies are carried out
exactly as above, e.g.
'Era fleghes war an kyttryn?' = 'Were there children on the bus?'
'Era.' = 'Yes, (there were).'   'Nag era' = 'No, (there were not)'

8.

Where you will be; what you will be doing.

Although there is a form for this, Colloquial Cornish only makes use of the Present - as often the case in English. e.g. 'Will you be going tomorrow?' = 'Are you going tomorrow?'. However, the form is given here for those who wish to use it.

Statements		Negatives	
y fydhaf-vȳ	= I will be	Ny vydha'vȳ = I will not be	
y fydh'ta	= you will be (s)	Ny vydh'ta = you will not be	
y fyth-ef	= he will be	Ny vyth-ef	etc.
y fyth-hȳ	= she will be	Ny vyth-hȳ	etc.
y fydhyn-nȳ	= we will be	Ny vydhyn-nȳ	
y fydhough-whȳ	= you will be (p)	Ny vydhough-whȳ	
y fyth an jȳ	= they will be	Ny vyth an jȳ	
y fyth an dēn	= the man will be	Ny vyth an dēn	
etc.	etc.	etc.	

Questions

The questions are formed exactly like the negatives, only the 'Ny' being replaced by 'a'
e.g. 'a vyth ef yn Por'Ya?' - 'Will he be in St. Ives?'

Replies

Replies to questions follow the exact pattern as before only with the exception that in the negative 'Nag' becomes 'Na'.
E.g. 'A vydh'ta ow mōs?' = 'Will you be going?'
'Na vydhaf' = 'No (I won't)
● In the affirmative replies the initial f/v starting the verb (y fyth ef, ny vydha'vȳ, etc.) changes to 'B'
E.g. 'A vydh'ta ow mōs?' - 'Will you be going?'
'Bydhaf' - 'Yes (I will).

● **Y fyth**   Again this has a second meaning -'There will be'. E.g. 'Y fyth bara avorow'-'There will be bread tomorrow.'
And of course, there are negatives and questions:
'Ny vyth'- 'there won't be'.
'A vyth'- 'will there be?'
E.g. 'A vyth glaw avorow?' - 'Will there be rain tomorrow?'
'Na vyth!' - 'No, (there won't be)'.

What you are ; how you are

Let us set out our columns again.

1

mȳ	:	I
tȳ (chee)	:	you (sing.)
ef	:	he
hȳ	:	she
nȳ	:	we
whȳ	:	you (plur.)
an jȳ	:	they
an dēn	:	the man
Jowan	:	John
an düs (deez):	:	the men
an wedren	:	the glass
an darras	:	the door

2

Yū am / is / are

3

squȳth	:	tired
dyek	:	lazy
avar	:	early
holērgh	:	late
lün	:	full
gwak	:	empty
rüth	:	red
glās	:	blue
gwydn	:	white
lōs (looz):	:	grey
gwēr	:	green
gell	:	brown

Again form sentences from the columns

● This form of the present tense of this verb can only be used as in these examples, i.e., to express the **condition** or **state** of something or someone, - 'the man is lazy; 'I am tired' etc. It **cannot** be used to express 'am', 'is' or 'are' when in the context of **position** or **action** as demonstrated on the previous pages. At first the difference may be difficult to appreciate, but with use the problem will disappear.
Examples to illustrate this further.

Correct

mȳ yū squȳth	:	I am tired
Theram ow mōs	:	I am going
Ma·hȳ y'n gegyn	:	She is in the kitchen

Incorrect

Theram squȳth
mȳ yū ow mōs
Hȳ yū y'n gegyn

More words

an bara	= the bread	ow tywrōsa	: cycling
an lēth	= the milk	ow treghy	: cutting
an coref	= the beer	ow clappya	: talking
an dewotty	= the pub.		and some words to tack
an gwerthjy	= the shop		on to the above columns :
an eglos	= the church	puppRȳs	: always
an carjy	= the garage	solabrȳs	: already
an cartan	= the car	arta	: again
an dhywrōs	= the bicycle	whāth	: yet, still.

Negatives

In place of columns 1 and 2 on previous page, insert this one column only:

Nyns oma	I am not
Nyns osta	you are not
Nyns yūa	he is not
Nyns yū hȳ	she is not
Nyns on nȳ	we are not
Nyns ough whȳ	you are not
Nyns yn jȳ	they are not
Nyns yū an dēn	the man is not
Nyns yū Jowan	John is not
Nyns yū an düs	the men are not
Nyns yū an wedren	the glass is not
Nyns yū an darras	the door is not

Questions

Very easy. Knock off the 'Nyns' for the open question, e.g.
'Yn jȳ avar?' = 'Are they early?'

Negative questions: Simply add 'a' in front of the 'nyns', left, for the negative question, e.g.
'A nyns yūa squȳth?' = 'Isn't he tired?'

Replies

The same pattern as before, i.e. for the negative replace the 'Nyns' by 'Nag' and drop the suffix, where applicable; and for the affirmative drop the 'Nag' above. E.g.
'Osta avar?' - 'Are you early?'
'Oma' - 'Yes (I am)'.
'Nag oma' - 'No (I am not)'.

Form sentences using the negative constructions combining the columns and new words on the previous page.
Now follow this by making sentences using the question pattern above and giving the appropriate answers (both negative and affirmative).
E.g. 'Yū an dēn fol?' = 'Is the man a fool?'
'Yū' = 'Yes (he is)'.
'A nyns yū an fleghes squȳth?' = 'Aren't the children tired?'
'Nag yū' - 'No!'

Pyth = what.

Another useful word for questions and very easy to use; just add it to the front of the question form without any other alterations.
e.g. 'Pyth erosta ow cūl?' - 'What are you doing?'
'Pyth yū lyw an darras?' - 'What is the colour of the door?'
● 'Lyw an darras' - '(the) colour (of) the door'

11.

What you will be; how you will be.

To describe what you will be, replace `yū` in the present tense on page 10 by `a vyth`. Thus,

`Mȳ a vyth squȳth` - `I will be tired`

Tȳ a vyth squȳth - `You will be tired`

etc., etc.

Negatives, Questions and Replies.

These are all formed in exactly the same way as set out on page 9 e.g.

`Ny vydha' vy` : `I will not be`

`A vyth ef claf?` : `Will he be sick?`

`Byth` - `Yes (he will be)`

This is the basic pattern for this verb and now we have seen how it works for the present tense (I am) and the future (I will be), the other common tenses will follow easily, because just as we formed the future by replacing `yū` of the present by `a vyth`, so we replace `yū` by other simple elements to obtain the English equivalents of `was`, `would be`, `have been`, `had been` etc.

What you were; how you were.

In Cornish we have **two** ways of expressing this.

1. As a **state** or **condition** - the man was sick; the bus was full; they were tired.

All we do here is to replace `yū` of the present tense by `ō`

E.g. `Mȳ ō squȳth` - `I was tired`

`Nȳ ō claf` - `We were sick`.

Negatives

Nyns ēna	=	I was not
Nyns ēsta	=	you were not (s.)
Nyns ōva	=	he was not
Nyns ō hȳ	=	she was not
Nyns ēn nȳ	=	we were not
Nyns eugh-whȳ	=	you were not (p.)
Nyns ō an jȳ	=	they were not
Nyns ō an dēn	=	the man was not
Nyns ō Jowan	=	John was not
Nyns ō an düs	=	the men were not

Questions & Replies.

These are all formed in **exactly the same way** as for the present tense

12.

Thus for example we have:
'ěsta clǎf dě ?' = 'Were you sick yesterday?'
'Nag ēna ' - ' No (I wasn't)'

Now construct your own sentences as you have been
doing, incorporating questions and replies on as
many topics as you are able.

2. As the result of an action — 'I was bitten by a dog';
   'the cake was cut by the bride'.

> For the statement, in place of 'ǒ' put 'vē'
> Thus:
> 'Mў vē brathys gen kў' - ' I was bitten by a dog'.
> 'An desen vē treghys gen an venen bryas' - 'The cake
> was cut by the bride'.

Negatives

Ny vēma	= I was not
Ny věsta	= you were not
Ny vēva	= he was not
Ny vě hў	= she was not
Ny vēn nў	= we were not
Ny vēugh why	= you were not
Ny von jў	= they were not
Ny vē an dēn	= the man was not
etc., etc.	etc., etc.

Questions and Replies.

Again these follow the
exact pattern as before
but note! the 'v' at
the beginning of the
verb changes to a 'B'
in the affirmative
answer, all as described
on page 9

Now, it is time to have some more words to widen
your vocabulary.

An trēn	= the train	ow hedhy	= moving
An gorsaf	= the station	ow casa	= leaving
An cay	= the platform	ow mūvya	= moving
An kў	= the dog	ow pyskessa	= fishing
cath	= a cat	ow palas	= digging
An gath	= the cat		
An strayl	= the mat	brathys	= bitten
fenester	= a window	treghys	= cut
An yet	= the gate	ledhys	= killed
An tō	= the roof	dybrys	= eaten
An fos	= the wall	tewlys	= thrown
An kē	= the hedge	terrys	= broken

What you would be

Again just a simple substitution!   Replace `vē` by `a vȳa`
e.g.
'Mȳ a vȳa squȳth wosa hedna' - 'I would be tired after that!'
'Ef a vȳa lowen dhe glewes hedna' - 'He wǒuld be happy to
                                        hear that!'

Negatives

Ny vȳen vȳ	= I would not be
Ny vȳes ta	= you would not be
Ny vȳa ef	= he would not be
Ny vȳa hȳ	= she would not be
Ny vȳen nȳ	= we would not be
Ny vȳeugh whȳ	= you would not be
Ny vȳa an jȳ	= they would not be
Ny vȳa an dēn	= the man would not be
etc., etc.	

Questions & Replies

Again exactly the
same

● Don't forget to
change the 'v'
to a 'B' where
applicable!

Where you had been; what you had been doing.

Simply change `a vȳa` to `re bȳa`
e.g.
'Tȳ re bȳa dhe Gambron' - 'You had been to Camborne'.
'Nȳ re bȳa ow quary sethȳgow' - 'We had been playing darts!'

> Negative and Question forms are the same as for
> 'would be' above because 'RE' only occurs in
> affirmative statements.

Where you have been; what you have been doing.

This time replace `vē` on the previous page by `re bē`
e.g. 'An jȳ re bē ow Kerdhes' - 'They have been walking!'
            (Kerres)

As before, because 're' is only used in affirmative
statements, the negative and question forms are
exactly as for 'vē'
e.g.
'Mȳ re bē dhe Bensans' - 'I have been to Penzance!'
'A vēs ta ena?' - 'Have you been there?'
'Bē ma' - 'Yes'
'Na vē ma - 'No'
● Don't forget the 'B' in the affirmative answer!

● **Note!** when you wish to ask **where** you have or had been, use 'PLĒ' exactly as you learnt on page 7, but remember to change the initial 'B' or 'V' to 'F' e.g.

'Plē ſēs ta?' - 'Where have you been?'

● This is the end of the section on the verb 'to be' in which all the common tenses have been introduced. Ensure that you have fully mastered them before moving on.

Vocabulary

An hanaſ	= the cup	tērnos	= next day
An tān	= the fire	tērnos vyttyn	= tomorrow morning
An gadar	= the chair	dē	= yesterday
blejen	= a flower	hedhyu	= today
an vlejen	= the flower	hedhyu vyttyn	= this morning
blejennow	= flowers	avorow	= tomorrow
when	= weeds	seythen	= a week
gweras	= soil	an seythen-ma	= this week
gwels	= grass	an seythen yu	
an gwels	= the grass	passyes	= last week
bownder	= lane		= next week
an vownder	= the lane	bledhen	= a year
an mor	= the sea	blōth (blooth)	= years old
an trēth	= the beach	hevleny	= this year
tewas	= sand	warleny	= last year

And now some revision!

Give the English for the following:

1. Theram ow palas y'n lowarth (looar)
2. Üsy Jowan ow mōs hedhyu?
3. An düs re bē dhe Redruth
4. Plē thera hȳ dē?
5. An kȳ vē ledhys gen an cartān
6. Tȳ yü squȳth hedhyu vyttyn
7. Ny vyth bara y'n gwerthjy avorow.
8. An jȳ re bē ow labma war an blejennow
9. Thera an jȳ ow prenassa y'n drē dē
10. Jory ō holergh hedhyu vyttyn

15.

what you do

There a number of ways in which simple verbal statements such as 'I see', 'You hear', 'The men shout', etc. can be expressed in Cornish, but here in **Everyday Cornish** we will only concern ourselves with the basic and most common way of expressing them. This method is through the use of the auxiliary verb 'do' - i.e. 'I do see', 'You **do** hear', etc. Let us set out our columns again.

1

Mӯ	=	I
tӯ (chee)	=	you (s.)
ef	=	he
hӯ	=	she
nӯ	=	we
why	=	you (p.)
an jӯ	=	they
an den	=	the man
Jowan	=	John
an dūs	=	the men

2

a wra

= do/does

3

dybry	=	eat
eva	=	drink
scryfa		write
potya	=	kick
sewya	=	follow
terry	=	break
megy	=	smoke
cafos		find / have / get

4

kӯk	=	meat
lyther	=	letter
tē	=	tea
coffy	=	coffee
oy	=	egg
an tresor	=	the treasure
an bēl	=	the ball

5

yn fenough	=	often
puptēth	=	everyday
trawythyow	=	sometimes
scantlowr	=	hardly

Now link these up as before, making as many sentences as you can, incorporating where possible all the columns.

E.g. 1+2+3+4+5 - 'Mӯ a wra dybry kӯk puptēth' - 'I eat meat everyday.'

Negatives

Here, as before, we must combine Columns 1 & 2

Ny wrama	=	I don't	Ny wreugh why	=	you don't (p.)
Ny wrēta	=	you don't (s.)	Ny wron jӯ	=	they don't
Ny wra va	=	he doesn't	Ny wra an dēn	=	the man doesn't
Ny wra hӯ	=	she doesn't	Ny wra Jowan	=	John doesn't
Ny wren nӯ	=	we don't	Ny wra an dūs	=	the men don't

Again link up your columns to give negative statements.
E.g.

'Ny wrama ēva coffy' - 'I don't drink coffee'
'Ny wra an düs dybry kȳk' - 'The men don't eat meat'

Questions

Just as we learnt earlier in the book.
Replace 'Ny' in the negative statement by 'a'
E.g.

'A wrēta ēva tē?' - 'Do you drink tea?'

Negative questions likewise follow the same pattern as before - place the letter 'a' in front of the negative statement.
E.g.

'A ny wra hȳ cana?' - 'Doesn't she sing?'

Replies

For the affirmative replies alter the negative column thus:

		Negative replies. As with previous exercises. Replace 'Ny' by '**Na**' and drop the suffix 'hȳ', 'nȳ' etc. where applicable. E.g.
Gwrama	= I do	
Gwrēta	= you do (s.)	
Gwra	⎰ he does ⎱ she does the man does John does the men do	'A wron jȳ cana?' - 'Do they sing?' 'Na wrons' - 'No (they don't)' 'A ny wra an dēn ēva coffy?' - 'Doesn't the man drink coffee?'
Gwren	= we do	
Gwreugh	= you do (p.)	
Gwrons	= they do	'Na wra' - 'No (he doesn't)

● Note in the affirmative replies that the letter 'G' starts the word. This is simply because there is no 'a' or 'Ny' at the start of the sentence.

Now construct sentences using statements, questions and replies as appropriate. Be sure you master the constructions, as they are the basic forms for all the different tenses and verbs that follow.
E.g.

'A ny wra Jowan dybry bara' - 'Doesn't John eat bread?'
'Na wra. A wrēta?' - 'No. Do you?'
'Gwrama' - 'Yes (I do)'.

17.

what you did

Now that you have fully mastered the basic construction set out on the last two pages, these next forms will be very simple for you as they don't amount to much more than substitutions. Thus, to change 'what you **do**' to 'what you **did**', simply alter 'a wra' in column 2 (page 15) to ' **wrǔk** ' (wrig) And that's it!
So now we have
  'Mȳ wrok dybry kȳk puptěth'   - ' I did eat meat everyday.'

Negatives
Again we have to learn these for each person and here they are

Ny wrǔgavȳ	=	I didn't
Ny wrǔssta	=	you didn't (s.)
Ny wrǔge	=	he didn't
Ny wrǔk hȳ	=	she didn't
Ny wrǔssyn nȳ	=	we didn't
Ny wrǔssough whȳ	=	you didn't (p.)
Ny wrǔg an jȳ	=	they didn't
Ny wrǔk an děn	=	the man didn't
etc., etc.,		etc., etc.

Questions and Replies. These are formed in exactly the same manner as before.
e.g.
  ' A wrǔge mōs?'
  = 'did he go?'
  'Na wrǔk - ' No.'
  'Gwrǔk' - 'Yes'

● Don't forget the 'G' in front of the affirmative, which applies to all persons of course.

'Pandra'- 'What'

This replaces 'Pyth', which is only used with the verb 'to be' (is, was, will be, etc.)
E.g. 'Pyth yw an lyw?' - 'What **is** the colour?'
  ' Pandr'**a wrěta** ěva?' -'what **do** you drink?'

Construct sentences, including questions and replies where appropriate, as before.

What you have done

Very simple. Put the little word '**Re**', which we have already met, in front of '**wrǔk**' and that's all!
Thus:
  'Mȳ wrǔk mōs' - ' I did go'.
  'Mȳ **re** wrǔk mōs' - ' I have gone.'
When we come to Negatives, Questions and Replies, the '**re**' disappears, just as we learnt on page 14 in connection with 'have been', 'had been', etc.

What you would do; what you had done.

Again very simple. For 'what you **would do**, replace `wrŭk` on the previous page by `a wrŭssa`. Thus
'Mȳ a wrŭssa cana' - 'I would sing'.
'Jowan a wrŭssa dōs' - 'John would come.'

For what you **had done**, again make use of the little word 'RE' as before, substituting it for 'a' in the above. Thus we have:
'Mȳ **re** wrŭssa dybry an desen' - 'I had eaten the cake.'

Negatives.

Both 'would do' (a wrŭssa) and 'had done' (re wrŭssa) have the same negative form because as you have already learnt 're' is not used negatively. And so setting out our negative column again we have:

Ny wrŭssen vȳ	= I would not / had not	
Ny wrŭsses ta	= you (s.)	
Ny wrŭssa ef	= he	etc.
Ny wrŭssa hȳ	= she	
Ny wrŭssen nȳ	= we	etc.
Ny wrŭsseugh why	= you (p.)	
Ny wrŭssa an jȳ	= they	etc.
Ny wrŭssa an dēn	= the man	
etc., etc.	etc.	

Questions & Replies

Just as you would expect. These are carried out in exactly the same manner as before, — But - don't forget the 'G' at the start of the affirmative answers.

● These last four pages have dealt with the most common tenses, enabling you to cope with most situations in an elementary conversation. You will have noticed that no **future** tense has been included however. This is simply because there is none in this form in Cornish. When you wish to say 'I shall go tomorrow' in colloquial Cornish, you use the auxiliary `**vedn**`, described fully on the next page.
E.g.
'I shall go tomorrow' - 'Mȳ a **vedn** mōs avorow.'

A few more words to finish the page

park	= field	an vrē	= the hill	aras	= to plough
prās	= meadow	an nans	= the valley	gonys	= to till
forth	= road	an vŭgh	= the cow	godra	= to milk
stret	= street	an tarow	= the bull	gweles	= to see

What you want to do; what you will do.

Statement
Replace Column 2 on page 16 ('a wra') by **a vedn**
You can now create sentences using the column patterns given on that page, e.g.
'Mȳ **a vedn** dybry kȳk'
= 'I **want** to eat meat'
(or) I **will** eat meat'

● **Remember! This is used to represent the Future tense in colloquial Cornish**
'Mȳ a vedn mōs avorow'
- 'I will go tomorrow'

Negatives
Ny vedn'ma	= I don't want to , I will not.
Ny venta	= you don't want to, you will not. (sing.)
Ny vedn ef	= he doesn't want to, he will not.
Ny vedn hȳ	= she doesn't want to, she will not.
Ny vedn nȳ	= we don't want to, we will not.
Ny vednough why	= you don't want to, you will not (plur.)
Ny vedn an jȳ	= they don't want to, they will not
Ny vedn an dēn	= the man doesn't want to , the man will not.
Ny vedn an fleghes	= the children don't want to, the children will not.

Questions and Replies
The pattern learnt in the previous exercises still applies: E.g.
'A venta dybry an desen?' - 'Do you want to eat the cake?'
'Na vedn'ma' - 'No (I don't want to)'
'Medn'ma' - 'Yes (I do want to).'
● Remember in this verb to change the 'v' to 'M' in the affirmative answers.

What you wanted to do

To put the previous statement into the past tense, replace 'a vedn' by ' a venja'. Thus, substituting in our example at the top of the page, we now have
'My a **venja** dybry kȳk'- 'I **wanted** to eat meat'

Now construct your own sentences as before.

Negatives

Ny venj'ma	= I didn't want to
Ny venjes ta	= you didn't want to
Ny venja ef	= he didn't want to
Ny venja hȳ	= she didn't want to
Ny venjen nȳ	= we didn't want to
Ny venjeugh whȳ	= you didn't want to
Ny venja an jȳ	= they didn't want to
Ny venja an dēn	= the man didn't want to
etc., etc.	etc., etc.

Questions and Replies.

Again repeat the standard pattern:
'A venja ef dōs?'
'Did he want to come?'
'Na venja' - 'No'
'Menja' - 'Yes'
   But don't forget the change of 'v' to 'M' again in the affirmative replies

Some verbs for you

leverel	= to say, to tell			
crysy	= to believe	ladha	= to kill	
predery	= to think	ladra	= to steal	
nȳja	= to fly	gwary	= to play	
nūvya	= to swim	gwaynya	= to win	
būdhy	= to drown	kelly	= to lose	

What you can do

Another simple substitution! This time replace Column 2 ('a wra' or 'a vedn) by **a el**.

E.g. 'Mȳ **a el** dybry kȳk puptēth' - 'I **can** eat meat everyday.'

The same pattern as before applies to the **Negatives, Questions** and **Replies**. We need to do no more than compile Column I as usual to show the individual persons.

Ny ellam	= I cannot
Ny allosta	= you cannot
Ny el ef.	= he cannot
Ny el hȳ	= she cannot
Ny ellen nȳ	= we cannot
Ny ellough whȳ	= you cannot
Ny el an jȳ	= they cannot
Ny el an dēn	= the man cannot
etc., etc.	etc., etc.

Just to refresh our memories we will set out a couple of examples of Questions and Replies.

'A allosta clapya Kernewek?'
-'Can you speak Cornish?'
'Mȳ ellam'
(or) 'Gellam' } 'Yes (I can)'
'A ny el hȳ gwary?'
-'Can't she play?'
-'Na el' - 'No (she can't)
-'Gel' - 'Yes (she can)

● **Note!** As with 'Gwrama' 'Gwrūk' etc., the affirmative reply starts with a 'G'.

What you could do

To put our previous exercise into the past tense, replace `a el' by `a alja'.   Thus we have,
 `Mȳ a alja mōs'   - `I could go'.

And for our Negatives, Questions and Replies we will set out our column again :

Ny aljen vȳ	= I could not	**Examples of**
Ny aljes ta	= you could not	**Questions & Replies**
Ny alja ef	= he could not	
Ny alja hȳ	= she could not	`A ny alja an düs dōs?'
Ny aljen nȳ	= we could not	-`Couldn't the men come?'
Ny aljeugh why	= you could not	`Na alja' -`No'
Ny alja an jȳ	= they could not	`A aljes ta dybry an bara?'
Ny alja an dēn	= the man could not	-`Could you eat the bread?'
Ny alja an düs	= the men could not	`Mȳ aljen
etc., etc.	etc., etc.	(or) `Ꝯaljen' } `Yes'

● Don't forget the `G' again in the affirmative replies!

Who

There are two words in Cornish for `who'
 1. **Pyū**   2. **Nep**

The first is used only in **questions** such as :

`Pyū yū an dēn?'  - `Who is the man?'
`Pyū a vedn mōs?' - `Who wants to go?'

The second is used only in a **relative** sense and **never** in questions.
E.g.
`Ef yū an dēn **nep** a vedn mōs' - `He is the man who wants to go!'

The two **cannot** be interchanged.
Here is one further example to illustrate the point.

`Pyu yū an map **nep** wrük potya an bēl?'
`Who is the boy **who** kicked the ball?'

What you do to me, him, her, etc.

We have seen how easy it is to say in Cornish, 'You see the woman' - 'Tÿ a wra gweles an venen.' But how do we say 'You see her?' All we have to do is place the word 'her' = 'hÿ' between the 'tÿ a wra' and the 'gweles', i.e.

'Tÿ a wra **hy** gweles.'

Similarly, 'You see me' - 'Tÿ a wra **ow** gweles.'

Pronouns	
ow	= me
dha	= you (s.)
y	= him
hÿ	= her
'gan	= us
'gas	= you (p.)
'ga	= them

● There is one very important thing we must watch here however. Certain of these words **change** the first letter that immediately follows. This a facet of Cornish (in common with other Celtic languages) and something we must learn in due course. Don't worry at first if you forget to carry out this change or 'mutation' as it is called – people will still understand you. The words and the changes they affect are as follows:

ow, hÿ. 'ga.

c → h	'Tÿ a wra **ow** hara (cara)' - 'You love me'
k → h	'Mÿ wrük '**ga** helly (kelly)' - 'I lost them'
p → f	'An màp wrük **ow** fotya (potya)' – 'The boy kicked me.'
qu → wh	'Ef a el **hÿ** whetha (quetha)' - 'He can clothe her'
t → th	'An dèn a vedn '**ga** therry (terry)' - 'the man will break them.'

dha, y change

b → v	'Mÿ a vedn **y** vera (bera)' - 'I shall drop it.'
c → g	'Ny el an jÿ **dha** gregy (cregy)' - 'They cannot hang you.'
k → g	'A wrüssta **y** gelly? (kelly)' - 'Did you lose him?'
d → dh	'Jowan a venja **y** dhybry (dybry)' - 'John wanted to eat it.'
g drops out	'Hÿ wrük **y** ladnhē (gladnhē)' - 'She cleaned it.'
gw → w	'A el an jÿ **dha** weles? (gweles)' - 'Can they see you?'
ch → j	'Hÿ wrük **y** jervysya (chervysya) - 'she borrowed it.'
m → v	'A allosta **y** vūvya? (mūvya)' - 'Can you move it?'
p → b	'An jÿ wrük **y** botya (potya)' - 'They kicked him!'
qu → gw	'Mÿ a vedn **dha** gwetha (quetha)' - 'I will clothe you.'
t → d	'Ny wrüg an jÿ **y** derry (terry)' - 'They didn't break it.'

'gan , 'gas do not effect any change

● This format applies to **all** constructions we have learnt since page 16 - negatives and questions included, as on the previous page. All we do is to put the 'person' to whom the action is being done immediately in front of the main verb.

Study and **learn** the mutations and construct your own sentences in the same manner as those illustrated.

My, your, his, etc.

We use exactly the same words for 'my', 'your', 'his', etc. as we used for 'me', 'you', 'him', etc. in the previous exercise.
● They precede the noun they qualify and remember they can change the first letter of the word that follows.

ow **f**el	: my ball	Examples,
dha **b**el	= your ball	'Mȳ a el gweles **dha dās**'
y **b**el	= his ball	- 'I can see your father.'
hȳ **f**el	= her ball	
'gan pel	= our ball	'Tȳ re wrŏк dybry **ow thesen**'
'gas pel	= your ball	- 'You have eaten my cake'
'ga **f**el	= their ball	

During our earlier exercises in this book, we learnt different verbs and different forms of those verbs, each having a little suffix, such as 'y fydhaf **vȳ**', 'thera **nȳ**', 'ny wrŭg **an jȳ**'. These suffixes are used primarily to either emphasize the person to whom an action refers, or to clarify the particular person when there could be some confusion, e.g.

'Thera **ef**' - 'he was'
'Thera **hy**' - 'she was'

These little suffixes can be used also with the possessive pronouns given in this exercise to emphasize ownership, e.g.

'ow hath-**vy**' - '**my** cat'; 'y dās-**ef**' - '**his** father' etc.

In colloquial Cornish, the possessive pronoun itself ('ow', 'dha', 'y', etc.) is often left out and the little suffix only used. e.g.

'A wrēta cara chȳ-**vȳ**?' - 'Do you like **my** house?'
'Mȳ a venja gweles tās-**hȳ**' - 'I wanted to see **her** father.'
'Thera fleghes **an jȳ** yn Kembry - '**Their** children were in Wales.'

● Note! These latter constructions will **only** be found in colloquial Cornish.

Adjectives

These are words which describe something - i.e, 'a **red** book', 'a **white** horse', etc. In Cornish the adjective **follows** the noun - ' a book **red**', 'a horse **white**'. It was noted at the beginning of the book that **all** nouns are either masculine or feminine. This at first may seem of little relevance - particularly when we are talking of chairs, tables, cups etc. However, it will now be seen why we must know whether a particular noun is masculine or feminine. It is because of this 'mutation' or changing of initial letters of certain words in certain situations - introduced in the last exercise. This process may have been noticed before, only the learner thinking that there had been a misprint ('**Benen**' = woman, 'an **Venen**' = the woman). It is no misprint. These changes follow rigid rules ~ and some of these apply to the use of 'an' = 'the', before a noun, and adjectives (following the noun). Here is the rule :-

---

If a noun is **feminine singular** or **masculine plural referring to persons**, 'an' changes the initial letter of the noun following and this noun in turn effects the same change on the first or only adjective immediately following.

The letters changed are the same as those set out for '**dha**' and '**y**' on page 23.

Here is an example to clarify the above rule

Singular		Plural	
benen	= a woman	benenes	= women
an **V**enen	= **the** woman	an benenes	= **the** women
an **V**enen dew	= **the fat** woman	an benenes tew	= **the fat** women
map	= a boy	mebyon	= boys
an map	= **the** boy	an **V**ebyon	= **the** boys
an map tew	= **the** fat boy	an **V**ebyon dew	= **the fat** boys.

(No change in **masculine**)   (No change in **feminine**)

● The gender of the above examples is obvious, but a list of the nouns used in this book is given at the end.
● Using the list of adjectives given below, construct sentences to familiarise yourself with the mutation procedure.

tew	= fat	rych	= rich	da	= good
mōn	= thin	tryst	= sad	drōk	= bad
bōhosek	= poor	lowen	= happy	clāf	= sick
(brōjek)					

25.

'That'

There are certain verbs which are often followed by 'that'; e.g.

'I believe that..............', ' I think that...............',
' I hear that..............', 'He said that...............'

In colloquial Cornish there are two constructions used to convey this meaning, both equally simple to use.

1. E.g. 'I believe that he ate the cake'. We will re-write this first in another form :

' I believe **he to eat** the cake'

Now let us put this into Cornish by splitting up the sentence.
'I believe' - 'Mÿ a wra predery' (as we already know)
'he to eat' - 'ef dhe dhybry' - this the part we are concerned with.

'the cake' - 'an desen'

So looking at the 'he to eat' part of the sentence which typifies the construction, all we do is to say:

Subject - 'dhe' - verb-noun (ef - dhe - dhybry)

A further example to clarify any misunderstanding:-

'He said that he would write' Re-write this as before : 'He said **he to write**', and in Cornish : 'Ef wrük leverel **ef dhe scryfa**'

● Note! **'dhe'** mutates, as does 'dha' and 'y'.

2. The use of **'dre'** (often written and voiced as **'tel'** or **'tre'** before vowels)

This is very simple to use — as of course anything colloquial is. All we do is to put **'dre'** in the sentence as it is in English and follow it immediately with the relevant form of the verb as we learnt earlier.
E.g.
'I think that he did go'- 'Mÿ a wra predery **dre** wrüg e mōs.'
' He said that she was sick'- 'Ef wrük leverel **dr**'ohÿ clāf.'
' They saw that they were moving' - 'An jÿ wrük qweles **tel** era an jÿ ow mūvya.'

● The second alternative given here is **only** used in colloquial Cornish.
● Beware also! In English, 'that' in this context is not always present. E.g.,
' I think he is better' = ' I think **that** he is better.'

Prepositions

These are words that describe time, place, means, etc.
- In the house; **around** the corner; **through** the door;
with a book, etc.

We have met some of these words already - in the first
exercise. There we used them exactly as in English and as
demonstrated above. However, when we wish to use these
prepositions with persons we **cannot** use them as in English
by simply linking them with the pronouns - to **him**; by **her**
etc. Let us look at this more closely with some examples.

'Mȳ a wra scryfa **dhe**'n dēn   'Ef wrük dōs **gen** an lyver'
- 'I write **to** the man!'   - 'He came **with** the book'

'Thera vȳ **dhe**'n scol dē'   'An lyver **gen** Charles Dickens'
- 'I was **at** school yesterday'.   - 'The book **by** Charles Dickens'

Now linking **dhe** with persons: And linking **gen** with persons

dhym (or) dhe vȳ	=	to me
dhys	=	to you (s.)
dhodho	=	to him
dhedhȳ	=	to her
dhe nȳ	=	to us
dhe whȳ	=	to you (p)
dhe'n jȳ	=	to them

gen'ma	=	with me
genes	=	with you (s.)
gen ef	=	with him
gensȳ	=	with her
genen	=	with us
genough	=	with you (p.)
gens an jȳ	=	with them

Similarly,

'Hȳ wrük mȳras **ort**' an skesen'   'Ny wrügavȳ mōs **yn** kyttryn!'
- 'She looked **at** the picture'   'I didn't go **in** a bus'.

Now with persons: And with persons

ortyf	=	at me
ortys	=	at you (s.)
orto	=	at him
orty	=	at her
ortyn	=	at us
ortough	=	at you (p.)
ort an jȳ	=	at them

ynnof (or) ettof	=	in me
ynnos	" ettos	=	in you (s.)
ynno	" etto	=	in him
ynny	" ettȳ	=	in her
ynnyn	" etton	=	in us
ynnough	" ettough	=	in you (p.)
yn an jȳ	" et an jy	=	in them

More prepositions and their combinations together with rules
regarding their connection to verbs follow on the next page.

Rag - for

ragovȳ	=	for me
ragos	=	for you
ragtho	=	for him
ragthȳ	=	for her
ragon	=	for us
ragough	=	for you
rag an jȳ	=	for them

Dyworth (Durt) - from

durtam	=	from me
durtas	=	from you (s)
durto	=	from him
durtȳ	=	from her
durtyn	=	from us
durtough	=	from you (p.)
durt on jȳ	:	from them

a - of

ahanaf	=	of me
ahanas	=	of you
anodho	=	of him
anedhȳ	=	of her
ahanan	=	of us
ahanough	=	of you
anedh on jȳ	=	of them

● Note the difference between 'dhe' & 'ort', both meaning 'at' in English.

dhe means 'at' with respect to position — i.e., 'At school', 'at home' etc.

'**ort**' means 'at' in the sense of 'towards' — i.e., 'Look at', throw at' etc.

'Dhe' and 'ort' **must** follow certain verbs in Cornish, although their use may seem strange in English. The most common are:

Scryfa dhe	=	write (to)	kewsel ort'	=	speak (at)
leverel dhe	=	say (to)	pellgewsel ort'	=	telephone (at)
rȳ dhe	=	give (to)	govyn ort'	=	ask (at)
gweres dhe	=	help (to)	mȳras ort'	=	look at

There is another type of combination of preposition and pronoun and that is where the preposition is apparently split in two and the **possessive** pronoun (which we have already met) placed in between.

The most common is **Warbydn - against**. We will first use it with a noun :-

'Ef wrük potya an bēl warbydn andarras' — 'He kicked the ball **against** the door

And now combined with pronouns:

war **ow** fydn	=	against me
war **dha** bydn	=	against you
war **y** bydn	=	against him
war **hȳ** fydn	=	against her
war **'gan** pydn	=	against us
war **'gas** pydn	=	against you
war **'ga** fydn	=	against them

● Note! The possessive pronouns 'ow', 'dha', etc. change the first letter of the word following as we learnt on page 24. In fact the word is actually 'pydn', 'War' itself changing the 'p' to 'b'.

'Must' = Rēs yū

1

Statement.

Rēs yū dhym	:	I must
Rēs yū dhys	:	you must
Rēs yū dhodho	:	he must
Rēs yū dhedhy	:	she must
Rēs yū dhe nȳ	:	we must
Rēs yū dhe whȳ	:	you must
Rēs yū dhe'n jȳ	:	they must

2

mōs	:	go
dalleth	:	start
gorſedna	:	finish
caſos	:	have
assaya	:	try
parüsy	:	prepare
gül (geel)	:	do, make.

3

lebmyn	:	now
wharē	:	soon
on oberen	:	the job
powes	:	rest
aral	:	another
kydnyow	:	dinner

● Construct sentences using the combinations 1 + 2 + 3.

E.g. ` Rēs yū dhym mōs lebmyn.`

- ` I must go now `

` Rēs yū dhodho caſos powes `

- ` He must have a rest.

Negatives

Replace ` Rēs yū ` by `Ny rēs` , e.g.

`Ny rēs dhym ' - ` I must not `

`Ny rēs dhys ' - ` you must not

etc.   etc.

Questions and Replies.

For the Question replace `Rēs yū` by `yū rēs?` e.g.

`yū rēs dhe vȳ?' - `Must I?'

`yū rēs dhys?' - `Must you?'

Replies

Affirmative - `Yū'.

Negative - `Nag yū'.

'Shall have to'

statement

Replace `Rēs yū` by `Rēs vyth' - thus

`Rēs vyth dhym mōs'

`I shall have to go'

etc. etc.

Negatives

Replace `Rēs vyth` by `Ny vyth rēs'. e.g.

`Ny vyth rēs dhodho dōs'

- `He won't have to come.'

Questions - as you would expect - ` `vyth rēs?'

and likewise with **replies.**

`Byth'- Yes'; `Na vyth'- `No'

'Had to'

As you have probably guessed!

statement

Replace `Rēs yū' by `rēs ō'

Negatives

Replace `Ny rēs' by `nyns ō rēs'

Questions.

Replace `Yū rēs?' by `ō rēs?'

Replies

`Nag ō' - `No'; `ō' - `Yes'

● As you can see, this is really based on the verb `to be' which we learnt in the earlier pages.

29.

'Ought to' - 'Y côth'

Statement

Replace 'Rēs yū' on previous page by 'y côth'; thus:

Y côth dhym : I ought to
Y côth dhys : you ought to
Y côth dhodho : he ought to
etc. etc.

Negatives

Simply replace 'Y côth' by 'Ny gôth'. Thus:

'Ny gôth dhe vÿ' - 'I ought not'
etc. etc.

● Note! the 'c' is replaced by 'g' in the negative.

Questions and Replies

As you would expect - replace 'Ny' in the negative by 'a'. E.g., together with replies:

'a gôth dhe nÿ gül hedna?' - 'Did we ought (should we) do that?'
'Na gôth' - 'No'
'Côth' - 'Yes'

● In both the constructions of 'Rēs' and 'Y côth', the **negative questions** are formed exactly as we learnt earlier in the book. Simply place 'a' in front of the negative statements. E.g.

'A ny rēs dhym?' - 'Mustn't I?'
'A ny gôth dhodho' - 'Didn't he ought to? (shouldn't he?)

This one, that one; these, those

An dēn-ma	= this man	An venen-ma	= this woman
An dēn-na	= that man	An venen-na	= that woman
Hemma	= this one	An rē-ma	= these
Hedna	= that one	An rē-na	= those

1	2
Tÿ a el cafos	hemma
Nÿ wrük clewes	an desen-na
A allosta gweles?	an rē-ma
An jÿ a venja dybry	an kyHryn-na
P'ür üsy ow môs?	dha lyfrow
Thera vÿ ow mÿras ort'	hedna
A ellam assaya?	an rē-na

● Make as many simple sentences as you can by linking boxes 1 and 2 as appropriate

30.

'Let's' = 'Gwren-nȳ

'Gwren-nȳ môs' = 'let's go'.
'Gwren-nȳ dalleth' = 'let's start'.

Negative - 'na wren-nȳ'

'Na wren-nȳ môs' = 'let's not go!'
'Na wren-nȳ dalleth whâth'
    - 'Let's not start yet.'

Let me..........!

E.g. 'Let me go!'
     'Let me sleep' etc.

Gas vȳ dhe......

'Let me go' - 'Gas vȳ dhe vôs'
'Let me sleep' - 'Gas vȳ
            dhe gusca'
● Don't forget the 'dhe'
which can change the
first letter of the word
following.

Imperatives

These are a type of command,
such as: 'Wait!' 'Don't go!' etc. As usual we will treat this
in the simplest way, as we have done throughout this book.
So, in the singular, i.e. when you are addressing one person,

    'Gwra..........!' = 'Do..........!'
    'Na wra........!'   'Don't......!'

E.g.

    'Gwra gortos!' = 'Wait!'
    'Gwra dybry dha bôs!' = 'Eat your food!'
    'Na wra môs ena!' = 'Don't go there!'

    And in the plural:
        'Gwreugh!'
        'Na wreugh!'

E.g.

    'Gwreugh tewlel hedna dhe-vês!' 'Throw that away!'
    'Na wreugh gwary ena!' - 'Don't play there!'

'Too; too much; too many' = 'Rē'

'Rē', which means all three of the above, is simply placed
directly before the word it qualifies, but **note!** it changes
the first letter of the word immediately following, in the
same manner as 'dha' and 'y' on page 23.

Examples

'An chȳ yu rē vras (vrawz)' - 'The house is too big'.
'Tȳ re wrük eva rē   - 'You have drunk **too much.**'
'Thera rē war an trên' - 'There were **too many**
                        on the train!'

Numbers

1.	ȳdn, onen
2.	deu (masc.)
	dyw (fem.)
3.	trȳ (masc.)
	tȳr (fem)
4.	pajer (masc.)
	peder (fem.)
5.	pymp
6.	whēgh
7.	sēth
8.	ēth
9.	naw
10.	dēk
11.	ȳdnek
12.	deudhek
13.	tredhek
14.	pejwordhek
15.	pemthek
16.	whētek
17.	sētek
18.	ētek
19.	nawnjek
20.	ügans (iggans)
21.	onen warn ügans
22.	deu) dyw) warn ügans
23.	trȳ) tȳr) warn ügans
	etc. etc.

● Numbers precede the noun as in English but take a **singular** noun, i.e. 'Pymp dēn' - 'Five men' **not** 'pymp tüs'

● 'ȳdn' is used with a noun as in 'one dog,' 'one house' etc. 'onen' stands alone.

● 'Two,' 'three' and 'four' have masculine and feminine forms, i.e., '**pajer** dēn' - 'four men' '**peder** benen' - 'four women.'

● 'Two' and 'three' cause the initial letter of the following noun to change.
'Deu' and 'Dyw' as 'y' (his)
'Trȳ' and 'Tȳr' as 'ow' (my)
e.g. 'Deu **dhen** ha dyw venen;
-'two men and two woman'
-'Trȳ **hȳ** ha tȳr **hath**;'
- 'three dogs and three cats.'

● But 'ȳdn' only changes the initial letter of **feminine** nouns
e.g. ȳdn dēn - one man
ȳdn venen - one woman

● 'An' = 'the' mutates 'deu & dyw.'
e.g. 'An **dheu** dhēn' - 'the two men'
'An **dhyw** venen' - 'the two women.'

● 'Mȳl' = thousand, changes or mutates as does 'y' (his)

From **30** onwards there are **two** forms, the traditional method reckoned in twenties, and the new, in tens.

Traditional

30.	dēk warn ügans	60	Trȳ ügans
31.	ȳdnek warn ügans	70	Dēk ha trȳ ügans
32.	deudhek warn ügans	80	Pajer ügans
	etc.	90	Dēk ha pajer ügans
40.	deu ügans	100	cans
41.	ȳdn ha deu ügans	200	Deu cans (no mutation)
42.	deu ha deu ügans	300	Trȳ hans
	etc.	400	Pajer cans
50.	dēk ha deu ügans	1,000	mȳl
	(or) hantercans.	1,000,000	mȳlvȳl

New form

30	Trўdek	60	whēghdek
31	Trўdek ўdn	70	sēthdek
32	Trўdek deu	80	ēthdek
	etc.	90	nawdek
40	Pajerdek	100	cans.
41	Pajerdek ўdn	200	
42	Pajerdek deu	300	
	etc.	400	} All as the traditional numbers.
50	Pympdek	1,000	
		1,000,000	

1st., 2nd., 3rd. etc.

1st.	Kensa
2nd.	Nessa
3rd.	Tressa (Truja)
4th.	Peswordha
5th.	Pympes
6th.	Wheghes

7th onwards, simply add 'ves' to the cardinal numbers you learnt on the previous page.
e.g. 8th. 'Ēthves'
9th. 'nawves'
16th. 'whētegves

After '20th.' - 'ügansves', numbers continue:
21st. 'kensa warn ügans'; 22nd. 'Nessa warn ügans', etc.

After '30th', the traditional form continues in the same way, i.e. '30th.' - 'degves warn ügans'; 40th. - 'deu ügansves'
41st - 'kensa war deu ügans', etc., etc.

After '30th', the New form continues as Noun + number, i.e. '31st man' = 'an dēn trўdek ўdn.'
'the 54th house' = 'an chŷ pympdek pajer.'

'Than' = 'es'

'An māp yū brassa es an vowes'.
- 'The boy is bigger than the girl'.
'An howl yū brassa es an lor'.
' The sun is bigger than the moon

If you wish to follow 'than' with a verb, then you must follow 'es' with 'del' and the 'personal' form of the verb we learnt as in Negatives etc.
e.g. 'He is bigger than you think'
- 'Ef yū brassa es del wrēta predery

Like 'dhe' and 'gen' etc., 'es' in the form 'ages' combines with pronouns.

agesof vŷ	=	than me
agesos ta	=	than you
agesso ef	=	than him
agessy hŷ	=	than her
ageson nŷ	=	than us
agesough-whŷ	=	than you
ages an jŷ	=	than them

E.g. 'Hŷ yū brassa agesof vŷ'
- 'she is bigger than me'.

33.

'As.............as' = 'Mar..............avel' ('vel)

'As white as snow' - 'Mar wydn avel ērgh
'Jowan yu mar vras avel Pedyr ' - ' John is as big as Peter'.
   (vrawz)

● Note 'Mar' mutates as does 'y' (his)
And as you might have guessed 'avel' also combines with
pronouns, thus:

avelof vȳ	= as me	
avelos ta	= as you	words
avello ef	= as him	brassa = bigger
avelly hȳ	= as her	gweth
avelon nȳ	= as us	lacca — worse
avelough whȳ	= as you	bras (brawz) = big
avel an jȳ ——— = as them		byghan = small
		mür = great
'Mȳ yu mar gōth avelosta		pōs = heavy
-'I am as old as you'.		scaf = light

● Now make up your own sentences with the help of the new
words given above.

Long, longer, longest.

This is known as the 'comparison' of adjectives and the
two basic ways of forming them in Cornish are as follows :

1. **Short adjectives** (usually those of one syllable)

   Hȳr   - Long
   Hyrra   - Longer (Double last letter and add 'a'.
   An hyrra - Longest (Put 'An' in front of above form)

● The 'hyrra' may precede or follow the noun , e.g.
   'An hyrra mȳldȳr (moldeer) }
   'Mȳldȳr an hyrra   } the longest mile.

2. **Longer adjectives**   For these the English equivalents
   'more' (**moy**) and 'most' (**an moyha**) are used.

   üghel   = high → 'Tour üghel' -' a high tower'
   Moy üghel   = higher → ' Tour moy üghel -' a higher tower'
   An moyha üghel = highest → ' Tour an moyha üghel'
                              -' The highest tower'.

Time of Day

Pȳ ür yū? Pyth yū an ür? }	what time is it?
Ȳdn ür yū	it's one o'clock
Dyw ür yū	it's two o'clock
Tȳr ür yū	it's three o'clock
etc.	etc.
Hanter wōsa (wuja)	half-past
Hanter wōsa pymp	half-past five
Quarter wōsa	quarter-past
Quarter wōsa sēth	quarter past seven
Quarter dhe	quarter to
Quarter dhe bymp	quarter to five.
Pymp mynysen dhe	five minutes to
Ogas dhe	nearly
Ogas dhe beder ür	nearly four o'clock
Ynter	between
Ynter pymp ha dēk wōsa ēth	between five and ten past eight.
Hanterdēth	mid-day
Hanternōs	midnight

● Don't forget that `dhe` can change the next letter.

Days of the week.

dē Sül (dē Zeel)	▪	Sunday
dē Lün	=	Monday
dē Merth	=	Tuesday
dē Mergher	=	Wednesday
dē Yow	=	Thursday
dē Gwener	▪	Friday
dē Sadorn	=	Saturday

Seasons, festivals.

Gwaynten	▪	spring
Hāf	=	Summer
Kydnyaf	▪	Autumn
Gwāf	▪	Winter
Pask	=	Easter
Golowan	=	Mid-summer
Nadelek	=	Christmas

Months of the Year

Mȳs Genver	▪ January		Mȳs Gortheren (Gorefan)	ꞏ	July
Mȳs Whevrer (Whevral)	= February		Mȳs Ēst	=	August
Mȳs Merth (Mer'h)	= March		Mȳs Gwydngala	▪	September
			Mȳs Hedra	▪	October
Mȳs Ebrel	= April		Mȳs Dū	=	November
Mȳs Mē	▪ May		Mȳs Kevardhū	=	December
Mȳs Metheven (Efan)	= June				

35.

what you have got.

'I have got' - that is, 'I own' or 'I possess', is
ma dhym, (or) **ma dhe vy**

similarly
ma dhys : you have got
ma dhodho : he has got
etc. etc.

E.g.
ma dhe vy ky ⎱
ma ky dhe vy ⎰ I have a dog

negatives
nyns üs dhe vy : I haven't got
nyns üs dhys : you haven't got
etc. etc.

E.g.
'Nyns üs ky dhe vy' : 'I haven't got a dog.'

Questions
'Üs dhym (dhe vy) : 'Have I got?'
'Üs dhys?' : 'Have you got?'
etc.
'A nyns üs dhym?' - 'Haven't I got?'

Replies
As we have already learnt,
i.e., 'Üs' - 'Yes'
'Nag üs' - 'No'.

What you have with you.

Here **dhym, dhys, dhodho** etc., is replaced by
'gen'ma' 'genes' 'gen ev' etc., e.g.,
'Üs arghans genes?'- 'Have you any money (with you)?'
Üs - 'Yes'
Nag üs - 'No'.

'ma ky gen'ma' - 'I've got a dog with me.'

● As you can see, the construction for the above is identical with that on the left, the only difference being that 'gen' is used instead of 'dhe'.

Adverbs
These describe the way in which you do something.

'I walk **slowly**'
'Do it **quickly**'

Basically the English adverb is formed by adding '-ly' to the adjective as above 'slow-ly', 'quick-ly'

In Cornish it is equally as easy. Simply put 'yn' in front of the adjective, i.e.,
'lent' - 'slow'
'yn lent' - 'slowly'
'scaf' - 'light'
'yn scaf' - 'lightly'
e.g.
'My a wra kerdhes yn lent'. - 'I walk slowly.'

Some link words
Ha	: and
mes (buz)	: but
bytegens	: however
ythō	: so, then
yndella	: thus
raghedna	: therefore
pella	: besides
martesen	: perhaps

Summary of Nouns, with genders & plurals.

Amary (m) amaryow	: Cupboard	Dywrōs (f) dywrōsow	: Bicycle
Arghans (m)	: Money	Eglos (f.) eglosyow	. Church
Bara (m)	: Bread	Ērgh (m)	: Snow
Benen (f.) benenes	. Woman	Fenester (f.) fenestry	: Window
Būgh (f.) bughas	: Cow	Flōgh (m) fleghes	: Child
Bledhen (f.) bledhennow	: Year	Fol (m) felyon	. Fool
Blejen (f.) blejennow	: Flower	Forth (f.) fordhow	: Road
Bownder (f.) bownderyow	. Lane	Fos (f.) fosow	: Wall
Bōs (booz) (m)	: Food	Glaw (m)	. Rain
Brē (f.) brēow	: Hill	Gorsaf (m) gorsavow	. Station
Cadar (f.) caderyow	: Chair	Gwels (f.)	. Grass
Carjy (m) carjyow	: Garage	Gwely (m) gwelyow	: Bed
Cartān (m) kerry-tān	: Car	Gweras (m) gwerajow	. Soil
Cath (f.) cathas	: Cat	Gwerthjy (m) gwerthjyow	. Shop
Cay (m) cayow	. Platform	Hanaf (m) hanavow	. Cup
Chȳ (chey) (m) chȳow	: House	Howl (m)	: Sun
Clēghy (m)	. Ice	Kē (m) kēow	. Hedge
Coffy (m)	. Coffee	Kegyn (f.) kegynow	. Kitchen
Coref (m)	: Beer	Kȳ (m) cün	. Dog
Darras (m) darrajow	: Door	Kȳk (m) kygyow	: Meat
Dewotty (m) dewottyow	. Pub	Kydnyow (m) kynyēow	: Dinner

37.

Kyttryn (m) kyttrynyow	: Bus	Powes (m)	: Rest
Lēth (m)	: Milk	Prās (f.) prāsow	: Meadow
Lyther (m) lytherow	: Letter	Seythen (f.) seythennow	: Week
Lyver (m) lyfrow	: Book	Skesen (f.) skesennow	: Picture
Lor (f.)	: Moon	Stevel (f.) stevelyow	: Room
Lowarth (loor)(m): Garden lowarthow		Strayl (m) straylyow	: Mat
Lyw (m) lywyow	: Colour	Strēt (m) stretyow	: Street
Māp (m) mēbyon.	: Boy, Son	Tān (m) tanow	: Fire
Meneth (m) menydhyow	: Mountain	Tarow (m) terewy	: Bull
Mor (m) morow	: Sea	Tās (m) tasow	: Father
Mowes (f) mowysy (moozy)	: Girl	Tē (m)	: Tea
Mōs (f.) mosow	: Table	Tewas (m)	: Sand
Mynysen (f.) mynys	: Minute	Tesen (f.) tesennow	: Cake
Mȳs (m) mysyow	: Month	Tō (m) tohow	: Roof
Mȳldȳr (moldeer) (m) myldȳryow	: Mile	Trē (f.) trevow	: Town
Nans (m) nansow	: Valley	Trēth (m) trethow	: Beach
Newl (m) newlow	: Fog	Tresor (m) tresorys	: Treasure
Oberen (f.) oberennow	: Job	Tour (m) tourow	: Tower
Oy (m) oyow	: Egg	Tȳak (m) tyogyon	: Farmer
Park (m) parcow	: Field	Whenen (f.) when	: Weed
Pēl (f) pelyow	: Ball		

38